This book
belongs to:

Text written by Gill Davies/Illustrated by Tina Freeman
First published in Great Britain in 2001 by Brimax
an imprint of Octopus Publishing Group Ltd
2-4 Heron Quays, London, E14 4JP
© Octopus Publishing Group Ltd

A Friend for Flash

B R I M A X READ WITH ME

A Friend for Flash

Flash feels lonely. He feels lonely because he is the only horse on Yellow Barn Farm.

"It is alright for those cows," he sighs. "There are lots of other cows in the field. They can all moo and play together all day long."

Flash wanders over to the next field.

"It is alright for those sheep," sighs
Flash. "There are lots of other sheep
in the field. They can baa and
play together all day long.
But I am the only horse."

Flash wanders over to the farmyard.

"It is alright for those geese," sighs
Flash. "There are lots of other geese
in the farmyard. They can honk
and play games all day long.
But I am a lonely, only horse."

Flash wanders back to his field. He thinks of all the other lucky animals on Yellow Barn Farm.

"There are lots of pigs to grunt together, lots of hens to cluck together, and lots of ducks to quack together. But there is only one of me!"

Tears start to fall from Flash's eyes.

Ben, the wise, kind scarecrow, sees Flash crying and peeps over the hedge.

"You're not the only one who is a lonely one," says Ben.
"I am the only scarecrow."

"True," says Flash, shaking his tears away.

"Cheer up," says Ben. "No-one needs to be lonely on Yellow Barn Farm."

"Really?" asks Flash.

"Of course!" says Ben. "You can be friends with all of the animals. You can play with the cows and the sheep, the geese and the pigs, the hens and the ducks, and all the other animals on the farm."

"And best of all," says Ben, "you can play with me! I have a broomstick leg and I can only hop about slowly, so you can give me rides."

Flash looks at Ben's one, wooden leg, and then looks at his own four, fast legs.

Flash knows just how lucky he is.

"Would you like a ride now?" asks Flash.

"Ooh, yes please," says Ben, and on he hops.

Now the two of them are great friends. Flash gives Ben rides every day as they visit all their new friends on Yellow Barn Farm.

Flash is never lonely now.

Here are some words
in the story.
Can you read them?

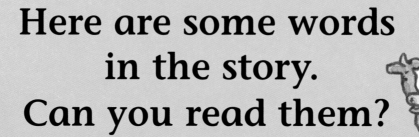

horse	geese
farm	pigs
cows	hens
field	ducks
sheep	tears
farmyard	scarecrow

How much of the story can you remember?

What sort of animal is Flash?

Why is Flash lonely?

What can the cows do all day long?

What can the sheep do all day long?

What can the geese do all day long?

Who peeps over the hedge to talk to Flash?

Who is Ben great friends with at the end of the story?

Help Flash to find a route
so that he can give Ben a ride.

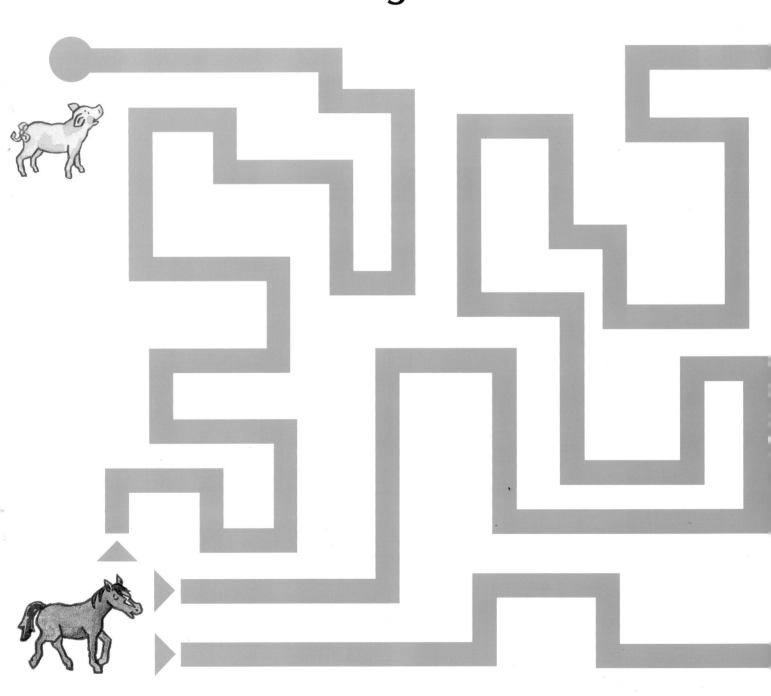

Notes for parents

The Yellow Barn Farm stories will help to expand your child's vocabulary and reading skills.

Key words are listed in each of the books and are repeated several times - point them out along with the corresponding illustrations as you read the story. The following ideas for discussion will expand on the things your child has read and learnt about on the farm, and will make the experience of reading more pleasurable.

• Talk about the many different noises and sounds that you can hear on Yellow Barn Farm in the morning. Make the different animal sounds and ask your child to point to the animal that they think makes the sound in the illustrations.

• Talk about all the sounds on Yellow Barn Farm at night. Can you hear any owls hooting or cats miaowing near your home at night? If possible relate the animals and objects seen in Yellow Barn Farm to real animals and objects in your child's daily life. Point them out to your child so they can bridge the gap between books and reality, which will help to make books all the more real!